Contents

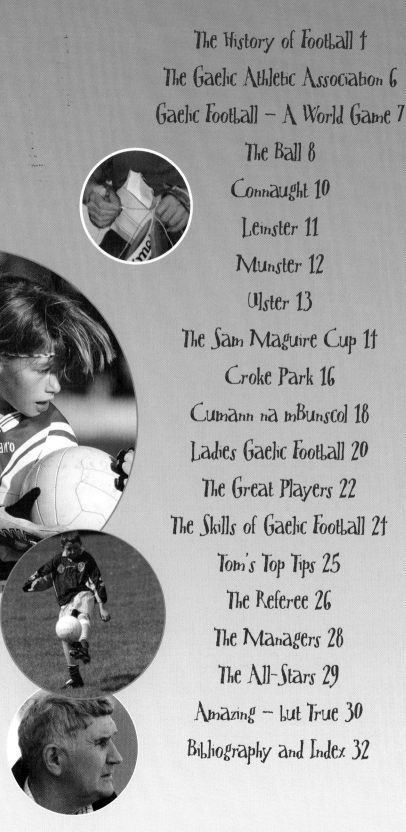

The History of Football

Gaelic football is a fast and exciting Irish field game.
There are 15 players on a team.
The ball can be kicked, hand-passed or fisted
into the opponent's net to score three points
or over a crossbar for one point.
Each game lasts 70 minutes with two halves of 35 minutes.
Gaelic football is played by men and women.

In the early years, various versions of the game
were played in different parts of the country.
The games were played between parishes
and would last for hours.
The number of players on each team varied from place to place.

Wrestling was part of the game in the early days.
Many people complained that the game was too rough
and wrestling was not allowed after 1886.

Eamon de Valera (later President of
Ireland) throws in the ball at a
final in Croke Park, 1920s.

There were 21
players on each team
for the first
All-Ireland in 1887.

For the All-Ireland of 1892 there were
17 players on a team.

A goal was equal to 5 points, but this was
reduced to 3 points in 1895.

In 1910 goal nets were used
for the first time.

In 1913 the number of players
on a team was reduced
to 15.

LIMERICK COMMERCIALS, ALL-IRELAND CHAMPIONS, 1887.

Limerick, first All-Ireland football champions, 1887.

In 1924 numbered jerseys were introduced.

The penalty kick was introduced in 1940.

In 1946 the side-line kick was brought in. Before that the ball was thrown in when it went out of play.

In 1980 play was extended to 80 minutes for All-Ireland finals, semi-finals and provincial finals.

Since 1975 all senior inter-county league and championship matches are 70 minutes long.

In recent years, players have been allowed take side-line kicks from the hand.

Since 1990 players have been allowed to take free kicks from the hand and side-line kicks must be taken from the hand.

Action between Kerry and Tyrone in Croke Park 2003.

The Gaelic Athletic Association

Gaelic football is organised by the Gaelic Athletic Association (GAA).
The first GAA meeting was held in 1884
in Hayes's Hotel in Thurles, County Tipperary.
Michael Cusack, a schoolteacher from County Clare,
was elected secretary. The first president was Maurice Davin.

The GAA was set up to organise Gaelic football,
hurling, rounders, handball and athletics.
The GAA had a wonderful influence
on the lives of Irish people.

In the first year, hundreds of clubs
were set up all over Ireland.
Until 1904, the winning club in each county
represented the county in the All-Ireland championship.
Limerick Commercials won the first
All-Ireland football championship in 1887.
Today a county team is selected from all county clubs.

Nowadays there are 2,500 GAA clubs in Ireland,
one in almost every parish.

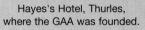

Hayes's Hotel, Thurles,
where the GAA was founded.

Action from a
Cumann na mBunscol
final in Croke Park.

Maurice Davin,
first President of the GAA.

The 1955 final between Kerry and Dublin.
Note the spectators sitting on the roof of the stand.

Gaelic Football – A World Game

When Irish people went to other countries
they took their national games with them.
Now Gaelic games are played in many different parts of the world.
There are 350 GAA clubs outside Ireland.

An All-Star exhibition game at San Diego, California.

- Nearly 4,000 players are registered in North America. They play in 93 clubs in 26 different cities.

- There are 50 clubs in New York and 13 in Canada.

- There are 88 GAA clubs in Britain; 38 of them are in London. There are 38 clubs in third-level colleges in Britain.

- 75 coaches teach Gaelic games in 65 schools in the West Midlands in England.

- Gaelic football has become very popular in Asia and it is played in China (Beijing and Shanghai), Hong Kong, Macau, Korea, Japan, Singapore and Taiwan.

- Children in Japan and Hong Kong are being coached in Gaelic football.

- There are 54 clubs in Australia and 10 in New Zealand.

- There are plans to start Gaelic football clubs in The United Arab Emirates (Dubai) and in Saudi Arabia, Malasia and Thailand.

- A European County Board was set up in 1999. There are now 17 European clubs, from Finland to Spain. A Euroleague is played across 8 European cities every year and is very popular.

An All-Star player enjoying the All-Star tour to Dubai.

The Ball

In the early days the ball was usually round
and coloured brown.
But sometimes it was oval-shaped
because footballs were difficult to make.
The ball was made of animal skin
with a pig's bladder inside.
When the bladder was inflated
the ball could be bounced.

The old brown ball soaked water
and got bigger from use.
It was difficult to catch when wet
and heavier to kick.

The old football was made of 12 leather sections.
A book written around 1720 says that
the ball, made of animal skin, was stuffed with hay
and could be kicked along the ground or in the air
and it could also be carried.

Today, adult players use a size 5 white football.
It weighs about the same as half a bag of sugar.
Count the panels on the ball and you should find 18 of them.
The 'bladder' inside is made of rubber.
The football does not soak rain-water
and the weight remains the same.

William Rock was known as the 'Custodian of the Ball'
in Croke Park. His job was to collect the balls for the matches
on the Friday before the game and have them ready.
On All-Ireland final days he wore a bowler hat
and he presented the ball to the referee on the pitch.
In wet weather the old balls became very heavy from the rain
and William threw in a new ball every 25 minutes.
Four of his sons, John, Charlie, William and Joe,
also worked in Croke Park. Joe Rock still looks after
the dressing rooms and his son, Joe, also works in the stadium.
William's son, Barney Rock, was one of the greatest forwards
ever to play for Dublin. He won All-Ireland minor
and senior medals and two All-Star awards.

Tom Grogan stitching ball panels at O'Neill's.

In 1932 a white ball was used for the first time in the All-Ireland final.

William Rock chatting with the referee before an All-Ireland final in Croke Park.

Good mentors and coaches make sure that each child makes contact with the ball 200 times during a well-planned training session.

'I would have worked a lot on my own with the ball out in the field. I spent hours and hours kicking and shooting. I used to spend hours and hours kicking the ball with my weaker left foot and I became confident using it to kick the ball.'

Tom Prendergast of Laois in *The Game of My Life* by Jack Mahon.

Connaught

GALWAY/GAILLIMH
In Galway, as in many other counties, the colours of the county champions were used originally. The changeover to the present jersey took place in 1936 and the crest was added about 1956. Maroon shorts are occasionally worn.
Main ground: Pearse Stadium

LEITRIM/LIATROIM
The present Leitrim colours date from about 1917, though white and green was sometimes worn in the 1920s. In 1927 when playing Kerry in the All-Ireland semi-final in Tuam, they wore the Dublin jerseys.
Main ground: Páirc Seán MacDiarmada

MAYO/MAIGH EO
Mayo's jersey had a v-neck style until the early 1950s when a white collar and cuffs were added. The crest was introduced in 1961. Green shorts are sometimes worn in place of white.
Main ground: McHale Park

ROSCOMMON/ROS COMÁIN
The Roscommon jersey was either black or white prior to 1938. Blue with a yellow band was also used. The present colour scheme was adopted for the 1943 final. Main ground: Dr Hyde Park

SLIGO/SLIGEACH
At one time the Sligo jersey was all black. A white band was introduced around 1925. Sligo was the only county to have an all black jersey. Since 1970 the county teams have been using a white jersey with black trim, black shorts and white stockings. Main ground: Markievicz Park

Leinster

CARLOW/CEATHARLACH
Up to 1910, Carlow used the colours of the county champions. In that year a set of green jerseys with red and yellow hoops was presented to the teams. These colours, with pattern changes, have been used since. Main ground: Dr Cullen Park

DUBLIN/BAILE ÁTHA CLIATH
Dublin wore the colours of the club champions up to 1918 when the sky blue shade with the crest was adopted. The change to the present kit was made in 1974. Main ground: Parnell Park

KILDARE/CILL DARA
The distinctive all-white of Kildare derived from the colours of the Clane club which won the county championship in 1903. Main ground: St Conleth's Park

KILKENNY/CILL CHAINNIGH
The familiar black-and-amber striped jersey originated in 1910 with the presentation of new jerseys to Kilkenny by John F Drennan. This settled a dispute which had arisen about the colours to be worn. Main ground: Nowlan Park

LAOIS
Laois changed from the colours of the county champions to a set of black-and-amber hoops in which they won their only All-Ireland senior hurling championship in 1915. The present blue and white were adopted in 1932. Main ground: O'Moore Park

LONGFORD/AN LONGFORT
Green and white hooped jerseys were used by Longford up to 1918 when a royal blue jersey with a gold sash was adopted. Around 1930 the sash disappeared but the gold trim was retained. Main ground: Pearse Park

LOUTH/AN LÚ
Louth have worn these colours since 1885. In 1957, when Louth won the All-Ireland, a St Brigid's Cross was presented to the team and the crest was included on the jersey in 1958. Main ground: O'Rahilly's Park

MEATH/AN MHÍ
A green jersey with a gold sash was used by the Meath team from 1908. The sash eventually disappeared, being replaced by the all green jersey with gold trim. Main ground: Páirc Tailteann

OFFALY/UÍBH FHÁILÍ
The national colours were very popular with clubs and counties in the early days of the GAA. Offaly earned the right to use them in Leinster as a result of a special competition. Several variations of the colours have been worn in recent years. Main ground: St Brendan's Park

WESTMEATH/AN IARMHÍ
Up to 1912 Westmeath wore a green jersey with a white loop, later changed to a maroon jersey with a saffron sash. The sash was dropped in 1936 and the present jersey has been used since. Main ground: Cusack Park

WEXFORD/LOCH GARMAN
In 1891 hurling final Wexford (Crossbeg) wore green and amber. In 1899 Blackwater represented the county wearing black and amber. Purple and amber was introduced in 1913. The placing of the colours has alternated over the years. Main ground: Wexford Park

WICKLOW/CILL MHANTÁIN
Bray Emmets were Wicklow county champions at the turn of the century. Wearing a green jersey, they won the All-Ireland club championship of 1901-02. The Wicklow inter-county team wore green until the early 1930s. Blue with a gold hoop was then used until the changeover to the present style in 1970. Main ground: Aughrim

Munster

CLARE/AN CLÁR

Tulla was the first GAA club to be established and the Clare jersey reflects this connection. Originally, the jersey was saffron with a blue sash, but around 1920 the present hoops replaced the sash.
Main ground: Cusack Park

CORK/CORCAIGH

Cork played in a saffron and blue jersey, with a large C on the chest, up to 1919. These jerseys were confiscated by British authorities and the County Committee borrowed a set of red and white jerseys. These colours were then retained. Main ground: Páirc Uí Chaoimh

KERRY/CIARRAÍ

Up to the 1903 All-Ireland football final, which was a draw, the Kerry colours were green and red, but were changed to green and gold for the replay when Kerry won their first All-Ireland title. The colours have been retained since then. Main ground: Fitzgerald Stadium

LIMERICK/LUIMNEACH

Limerick wore green with a white sash when winning the 1918 All-Ireland final but in the 1921 final wore green and white hoops. The present jersey was adopted about 1924.
Main ground: Gaelic Grounds

TIPPERARY/TIOBRAID ÁRANN

Up to about 1925 the Tipperary team usually wore the colours of the county champions. In 1925 the present gold hoop on a blue jersey was introduced. These colours reflected the influence of Tubberadora and other great Tipperary champions. Main ground: Semple Stadium

WATERFORD/PORT LÁIRGE

Waterford first took the royal blue of Munster with white collar and cuffs for its county jersey. In 1938 the jersey was changed to white with royal blue trim. In 1945, the Decies crest was added.
Main ground: Walsh Park

Ulster

ANTRIM/AONTROIM

The Antrim colours were adopted from the famous Shauns Club, and have been worn since inter-county football began except for a short period. Black shorts are worn on occasion. Main ground: Casement Park

ARMAGH/ÁRD MHACA

Up to 1926 Armagh wore the same colours as Kilkenny. In 1926 they played Dublin in the All-Ireland junior semi-final and wore jerseys knit for them by the nuns in Omeath in the colours that are used at present. Main ground: Athletic Grounds

CAVAN/AN CABHÁN

Royal blue has been used by Cavan since 1910. The white trim was introduced for the 1947 All-Ireland senior football final against Kerry, which was played in the Polo Grounds, New York. Main ground: Breffni Park

DERRY/DOIRE

Red was the traditional Derry colour. In 1947 Derry played in the National League final in a set of white jerseys with a red band. These colours have been worn since. Main ground: Celtic Park

DONEGAL/DÚN NA NGALL

Donegal have always worn green and gold. In 1966 they altered the strip to a gold jersey with green shorts, which they wore for a number of years. They have since reverted back to the green and gold jersey. Main ground: Mac Cumhaill Park

DOWN/AN DÚN

A red jersey was worn by Down up to 1922. From 1923 a blue jersey with white trim was worn. In 1933 Down changed back to an all red jersey but with black collar and cuffs. Black shorts were first worn in 1962. Main ground: Pairc Esler

FERMANAGH/FEARMANACH

Fermanagh originally used green and white hoops, the colours of the then county champions Treemore, which was the first club to be established in the county in 1901-02. Around 1934-35 a green jersey with yellow trim was used and this was later changed to white trim. Occasionally the county team wears a green jersey with red trim and red shorts. Main ground: Brewster Park

MONAGHAN/MUINEACHÁN

In Monaghan, up to 1913, the colours of the county champions were worn. Around 1920 the white jersey had a blue band added. Black and amber were used for a while in the mid-30s but in 1942 the original white with blue trim was reintroduced. Main ground: St Tiernach's Park

TYRONE/TÍR EOGHAN

The present Tyrone jersey has been used since about 1927. The crest is the Red Hand of the O'Neill clan whose family seat was at Dungannon. Main ground: Healy Park

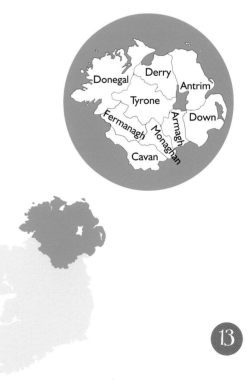

The Sam Maguire Cup

The Sam Maguire Cup is the prize
for the winners of the senior All-Ireland football final.
It is the most famous trophy in Irish sport
and has a magic all its own.
People from all counties love to see it,
touch it and be photographed with it.

It was first played for in 1928
when Kildare beat Cavan in Croke Park.
Bill 'Squires' Gannon was the first captain to receive it.
Kerry won it for the first time in 1929
and have won it more times than any other county.
Cavan were the first Ulster county to win it in 1933.
A Connaught county won for the first time in 1934
when Galway were victorious.

In 1960 the Sam Maguire Cup
was carried north by Down captain, Kevin Mussen.
Since then, Donegal, Derry, Armagh and Tyrone
have also won the famous trophy.

The Sam Maguire Cup is a copy of
the famous Ardagh Chalice.
It is 40.3cm high and has a diameter of 43.4cm.
It is made from silver and weighs 12 pounds (5.45 kilos),
but the base is over twice that weight at 28 pounds (12.72 kilos).
**Could you lift Sam Maguire over your head
after playing in an All-Ireland final in Croke Park?**

John Joe O'Reilly of Cavan was the only man to lift Sam Maguire outside Ireland. The 1947 All-Ireland final was played The Polo Grounds in New York. Cavan beat Kerry that unique final.

Tyrone Captain, Peter Canavan,
with the Sam Maguire Cup.

Sam Maguire

...s born of Protestant parents in ...nanway, County Cork. He worked in ...on and was very involved with the GAA. ...was a very good footballer and won three ...elands with London – in 1900, 1901 and 1903. ...e was captain of the team in 1901 and 1903. After his death, some of his friends gave the Sam Maguire Cup to the GAA so that his great work would be remembered.

Olambambi Fasanya, Holy Trinity School, Donaghmede, dreams of winning the All-Ireland one day.

The original Sam Maguire Cup was replaced in 1988 because it was damaged. It was put in the GAA Museum and the new cup was won for the first time by Meath. The captain, Joe Cassells, was injured and didn't play in the final but, luckily for him, the game ended in a draw and he was fit for the re-play.

Only 6 players have been presented with the Sam Maguire Cup twice: Joe Barrett (Kerry), Jimmy Murray (Roscommon), John Joe O'Reilly (Cavan), Seán Flanagan (Mayo), Enda Colleran (Galway) and Tony Hanahoe (Dublin)

Croke Park

The big GAA games are
held in Croke Park.
It is one of the biggest stadiums in Europe.
It holds 84,000 people and
has a wonderful playing surface.
It was bought by the GAA in 1913 for £3,500 (€4,444).

When it was refurbished recently it cost €200 million.

The Hogan stand is called after Michael Hogan.
He was the Tipperary goalkeeper in 1920.

The Cusack stand is called after Michael Cusack,
the teacher from Clare who was
one of the founders of the GAA.

Hill 16 was built using the rubble
from Sackville Street (now O'Connell Street)
which was destroyed during the 1916 Rising.

The Canal End stand is named
after the Royal Canal
which runs beside Croke Park.

16

Croke Park Time~Line

1908 – Frank Dineen bought the 'City and Suburban Racecourse' for £3,250.

1913 – The ground was bought by the GAA for £3,500 and named Croke Park.

1917 – Hill 16 was built.

1920 – Bloody Sunday happened.

1924 – The Hogan stand was built.

1924/28/32 – The Tailteann Games were held.

1938 – The Cusack stand was finished.

1949 – The Canal End was finished.

1952 – The Nally stand was opened.

1953 – American Football was played in Croke Park.

1959 – The Cusack stand was re-built.

1961 – The biggest attendance ever at an All-Ireland – 90,566.

1967 – The Galahs (Australian Rules footballers) played in Croke Park.

1972 – Mohammed Ali boxed in Croke Park.

1984 – International Rules Series was held.

1989 – Hill 16 was re-built.

1993 – Plans for the modern stadium were unveiled.

1998 – The Cusack Stand was opened. The Hogan stand and the Canal End development were officially opened.

2003 – The Special Olympics World Summer Games Opening and Closing Ceremonies were held.

Cumann na mBunscol

Most boys and girls first play Gaelic games in primary school.
Cumann na mBunscol – an organisation of primary-school teachers –
runs Gaelic football, hurling, camogie, handball,
rounders and athletics in 3,500 schools throughout the country.

Children take part in skill-training
and they play class leagues in the school yard.
They play friendly games and inter-county
challenge games with their schools.
Children get their first chance to wear their county jersey
when they play in Cumann na mBunscol games.
Nearly all county players played in
Cumann na mBunscol leagues.

Cumann na mBunscol is organised in all 32 counties.
Teachers encourage the children
to join their local GAA club.
There they can continue to play and enjoy Gaelic football.

The Dublin Cumann na mBunscol finals have been played in Croke Park since 1929. Gaelic games became more popular in Dublin after Cumann na mBunscol was founded in 1928. A group of teachers decided to start a league to encourage children to play their native games. Only eight schools took part in the first year.

In 1929 the children were invited to play their finals in Croke Park and a half-day from school was given to the teams and their supporters. This encouraged more schools to play and the league grew very fast. There are now hundreds of schools playing in Cumann na mBunscol competitions in Dublin and the finals are still played in Croke Park.

The INTO-GAA Mini-Sevens is a very popular national festival of Gaelic games and is run at county, province and national level. It starts as a competition in boys' and girls' Gaelic football, hurling and camogie. School winners in each county go to county finals and the winners then play in friendly festivals in their province.

Action from Cumann na mBunscol finals and the INTO-GAA Mini-Sevens 2004.

The very best players are selected to show their skills in Croke Park during the All-Ireland semi-finals and finals. Every year 240 boys and girls are chosen and it is a big honour for them. They march out on Croke Park behind the Artane Band and play for a short time on the field.

19

Ladies Gaelic Football

Cumann Peil Gael na mBan –
the Ladies Gaelic Football Association –
was founded in Hayes's Hotel, Thurles, County Tipperary, in 1974.
The growth of the organisation since then has been amazing.
There are now 90,000 members in 900 clubs
throughout Ireland and also in
Britain, Europe, Asia, Australia, Canada and the USA.

In 2004 the Ladies GAA launched their own coaching programme and their own magazine *Peil*.

There is an annual competition between the four provinces and an All-Ireland club competition.

Waterford's Caitríona Casey has won five All-Ireland medals with her county. She has three All-Star awards. She is a teacher in Dublin and has brought her school to 10 Cumann na mBunscol finals in Croke Park.

Cumann Peil Gael na mBan organises national competitions from under-14 upwards. There are competitions at junior, intermediate and senior levels and for secondary and third-level colleges.

An All-Star scheme was started in 1980. In 2004 the first All-Star tour went to New York where the All-Star team played a Rest of Ireland team in Gaelic Park before the Mayo v New York Connaught championship match.

Kerry won 9 All-Ireland senior titles in-a-row from 1982 to 1990.

Mayo Ladies Captain, Nuala O'Shea, lifts the Brendan Martin Cup in Croke Park.

Eight counties – Cork, Kerry, Tipperary, Waterford, Galway, Roscommon, Laois and Offaly – took part in the first All-Ireland senior championship in 1974. Tipperary won the final.

Mary Jo Curran (Kerry) has won the most All-Ireland senior medals. She has 9.

Mary Jo has also won the most All-Star awards.

21

The Great Players

Mick O'Connell

Mick O'Connell played for Kerry
in ten All-Ireland senior finals between 1959-1972.
Kerry won four of them.
Mick was only 22 years of age
when he was captain of the Kerry team
that won the All-Ireland in 1959.
He travelled home by train after the game
but left the Sam Maguire Cup in
the dressing-room in Croke Park!

Mick O'Connell was one of the best at catching the ball overhead and he was superb at kicking frees. He was one of the first superstars of the GAA.

Des Foley

Des Foley was captain of the Dublin minor
football team that won the All-Ireland in 1958.
He was captain of Dublin when they won
the 1963 All-Ireland senior football title.
On St Patrick's Day 1962, Des Foley set a record
when he won Railway Cup medals in football
and hurling for Leinster.

Munster Mick O'Connell
Leinster Des Foley
Ulster Peter Canavan
Connaught Seán Purcell

Maurice Fitzgerald

Maurice Fitzgerald is from Cahirciveen and was World Kicking
Champion in 1989. He beat the national champions of American
Football, Rugby League, Rugby Union, Soccer and Australian Rules
in Melbourne. He won All-Ireland medals in 1997 and 2000. He also
has 2 All-Star Awards.

Seán O'Neill of Down played for Ulster 26 times. He played in three
All-Ireland finals and won them all.

Peter Canavan

Peter Canavan was captain when Tyrone won All-Ireland under-21 titles in 1991 and 1992. He was captain of the Tyrone senior team that won the Sam Maguire Cup for the very first time in the All-Ireland of 2003. Peter Canavan scored 11 of 12 points for Tyrone in the 1995 All-Ireland final. Dublin scored 1-10 to win the title by a single point.

Through lots of practice, Peter could kick well and score with both feet. He played with great courage and he loved playing in the forwards.

Seán Purcell

Seán Purcell played for Tuam Stars and for Galway and was known as 'The Master'. He was captain of Galway in the 1959 All-Ireland against Kerry. Seán has one All-Ireland senior medal, 6 Connaught Championship medals, a National League medal, 3 Railway Cup titles and 10 County Senior Championship medals with his club.

Cork's Teddy McCarthy is the only player to win an All-Ireland senior football and hurling medal in the same year – 1990.

Mattie McDonagh

Mattie McDonagh of Galway is the only Connaught player to win 4 All-Ireland medals.

Kerry's Séamus Moynihan is one of the greatest players of modern times. He has won two All-Ireland medals. When Kerry won the All-Ireland in 2000, he was chosen as Footballer of the Year and the GAA Writers' Player of the Year.

The Skills of Gaelic Football

Catching the ball, kicking the ball and tackling
are the basic skills of the game.

Other skills include:
solo, pick-up, bounce, hand pass,
blockdown, free-taking and scoring.

'I can still
imagine that beautifu
feeling if you're comple
stretched looking up at
ball and nothing above
only the ball and the s
and you know you ar
going to get it.'
Jim McKeever
(Derry)

'I would spend
hours and hours
kicking the ball with my
weaker left foot. I became
really confident using it to
kick the ball.'
Tom Prendergast
(Laois)

'I used to train
non-stop. One of the
things I mastered was
picking up the ball while
sprinting without
breaking stride.'
Nudie Hughes
(Monaghan)

'Mick
O'Connell could
take frees, catch
the ball, kick right
and left.'
Johnny Geraghty

Tom's Top Tips

Tom Fitzpatrick.

1 Get your own size four football. Buy a pair of football boots. Get your own togs, socks and gloves.

2 Practise catching and kicking. Drop the ball from right hand to right foot and kick. Drop the ball from left hand to left foot and kick or solo. Practise soloing. When playing on your own always shoot for a target. Use your weaker foot a bit each day.

3 Always put your foot under the ball when picking up. Do it at pace.

4 Play fun games of football with your friends, practising skills in your local green. When playing a game never shout at your friends. It's only a game.

5 Invite your friends and your brothers and sisters to kick around with you. Why don't all of you join the local GAA club?

6 Play football at break time in school. Do your best to get on the school team.

7 Follow your county team and read all about the players in the newspapers and Gaelic magazines. Visit the GAA website at www.gaa.ie. Look in at www.cul4kids.ie also.

8 Tune in to live coverage of Gaelic games on TV. Visit Croke Park and experience a game played on the brilliant pitch. Drop in to the GAA Museum.

9 Be the best fan that your club and county could ever have.

'Your skills have to improve if you keep playing with the ball.'
Matt Connor (Offaly)

'You can develop skill over a period of time if you keep practising with the ball as I did.'
Mikey Sheehy

25

The Referee

No match can take place without a referee.
The referee awards frees when
rules are broken by players.
He is helped by his team of linesmen and umpires.
The referee wears an ear-piece
and is in contact with the umpires and linesmen during play.
It is a very important job
and can be a difficult one.
Referees do not get paid for the job
but they get great satisfaction from what they do.

To make his decisions clear to players and spectators,
the referee uses yellow and red cards.
The referee shows a yellow card
when a player is pulled down
or tripped by an opponent.
A yellow card is also shown for
other forms of rough play.
For striking, kicking, stamping
and behaving in a manner dangerous to another player
the referee shows a red card.

5 things
a referee must have:

1. a whistle
2. a watch
3. a pencil
4. a notebook
5. a coin

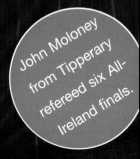
John Moloney from Tipperary refereed six All-Ireland finals.

Two former referees, Mick Loftus from Mayo and John Dowling from Offaly, became Presidents of the GAA.

Cumann na mBunscol teaches the rules of Gaelic football to many boys and girls.

They referee school and club games. These young whistlers enjoy the task. They are delighted with the chance to referee matches in front of large crowds during the summer months at big stadiums around the country.

The Managers

Mick O'Dwyer is the most successful manager
in the history of the GAA.
While he was manager of Kerry
they won 8 All-Ireland titles.
He then went on to manage Kildare.
In 1996 Kildare won a Leinster Championship
for the first time since 1956.
Mick O'Dwyer's next job as manager was with Laois
and they won the Leinster championship in 2003,
their first since 1946.

Kevin Heffernan won an All-Ireland senior medal
and three National League medals with Dublin.
He became manager of Dublin in 1973.
The following year they won the All-Ireland
for the first time since 1963.
He became a hero in Dublin
and the followers of the team
became known as 'Heffo's Army'.
His teams won All-Ireland titles in 1976, 1977 and 1983.

Seán Boylan from Meath was better known
as a hurler than a footballer when he was a player.
He was appointed manager of Meath in 1982.
They won the All-Ireland in 1987, 1988 and again in 1999.

Eugene McGee is from Longford.
His most famous game as manager was
the All-Ireland final of 1982
between Offaly and Kerry.
Offaly hadn't won the All-Ireland
since 1971. Kerry had won All-Irelands in
1978, 1979, 1980 and 1981.
Could they make it five-in-a-row?
No county had ever done that.
Kerry were hot favourites,
but Eugene McGee's team beat them.

Mick O'Dwyer

Kevin Heffernan

Seán Boylan

Eugene McGee

The All-Stars

The best players every year win All-Star awards.
Since 1971 the best 15 footballers have received an All-Star Award.
Four players have won awards in both football and hurling.
They are Jimmy-Barry Murphy (Cork), Brian Murphy (Cork),
Ray Cummins (Cork) and Liam Currams (Offaly).
Goalkeeper John O'Leary (Dublin) has won five All-Star awards.
Two other goalkeepers, Martin Furlong (Offaly) and Paddy
Cullen (Dublin), have won four each.
Offaly is the only county to have won All-Star awards in every
position on the field in both football and hurling.

Kerry's
Jack O'Shea
won six All-Star
awards in a row
from 1980 to
1985.

Offaly's Matt
Connor won three All-
Star awards (1980, 1982,
1983). The Walsh Island player also won a Leinster senior
medal and an All-Ireland senior
title. He was the top scorer in the
country for five successive years
(1979-1983) and scored a
total of 82 goals and 606
points in 161 games for
Offaly.

Kerry's
Pat Spillane
has most
All-Star
awards, 9
in total.

Amazing ~ but True

A very unusual game of football was played ON the river Liffey in 1740 when it was frozen to a depth of 6 inches (about 15cm).

Jack Murphy was one of the Kerry stars in the 1926 All-Ireland final against Kildare. He died of pneumonia before the replay. The trophy for the South Kerry championship is called after him.

Denis O'Sullivan of Kerry was the first player to play in All-Ireland finals in minor, under-21, junior and senior football in the same year, 1964.

Barney Royce of Wexford won All-Ireland medals in 1915, 1916, 1917 and 1918 as well as six Leinster Championship medals without ever playing in an All-Ireland or Leinster final. He was a sub in all of those games.

Wexford were trained to win the 1914 football final by boxer Jem Roche. A few years earlier Roche had fought Tommy Burns for the heavyweight championship of the world.

In the early years of the GAA, if a player put the ball over his own end-line his team's score was reduced by one point. This was known as 'a forfeit point'. Today a 45-metre free would be awarded by the referee.

In 1948 Pádraig Carney scored the first penalty in an All-Ireland final, Mayo v Cavan.

Galway lost All-Ireland finals in 1940, 1941 and 1942. Joe Duggan was on all three losing teams. In 1971, 1973 and 1974 his son, Jimmy Duggan, was on all three losing teams.

The only scoreless draw in inter-county GAA history occurred in the 1895 Munster final between Cor[k] and Kerry in Limerick. Wit[h] five minutes left in the gam[e] the ball burst and no repl[ace]ment could be found. T[he] referee decided that t[he] game was a draw.

The GAA All-Ireland championship medal is in the shape of a Celtic cross. It was copied from the design at the top of the ancient cross at Monasterboice.

The ball was thrown in from an aeroplane when Kerry played Dublin at the opening of Cusack Park, Mullingar, in 1934.

Wexford won four football finals in a row in 1915, 1916, 1917 and 1918. Kerry won four-in-a-row in 1929, 1930, 1931 and 1932 and again in 1978, 1979, 1980 and 1981.

Antrim were beaten 5-10 to 2-5 by Dublin in the 1907 All-Ireland semi-final in Dundalk. They had to dash to the station after the game in their playing gear to catch the Belfast train.

The first football match under GAA rules was between Callan and Kilkenny City on 15 February 1885 in Kilkenny.

In 1979 Eoin Liston of Kerry became the first man to score three goals in an All-Ireland football final.

Kerry's Mick O'Connell both scored and saved a penalty in the same club game.

Great footballers who never won an All-Ireland: Kevin Armstrong (Antrim), Pat Dunny (Kildare), Jim Hannify (Longford), Iggy Jones (Tyrone), Packie McGarty (Leitrim), Peter McGinnity (Fermanagh), Seán O'Connell (Derry), Gerry O'Reilly (Wicklow), Tom Prendergast (Laois) and Jimmy Rea (Carlow).

Four Delaney brothers played on the Laois team beaten by Mayo in the 1936 All-Ireland final. To add to the confusion for commentators, the brothers – Jack, Chris, k and Bill – had an uncle, m, who played at full-back. The goalkeeper was also a Tom Delaney.

Footballers who scored more than 100 points in a season: Matt Connor (Offaly) 1980/83, Dermot Earley (Roscommon) 1974, Michael Finneran (Roscommon) 1980, Charlie Gallagher (Cavan) 1965/67, Jimmy Keaveney (Dublin) 1975/77, Tony McTague (Offaly) 1971/73, Mickey Kearins (Sligo) 1965/68, Mick O'Dwyer (Kerry) 1969/70, Seán O'Neill (Down) 1968, Mikey Sheehy (Kerry) 1979.

Between 1975 and 982 Cork lost ight Munster enior football nals in a row to Kerry.

Eugene 'Nudie' Hughes managed to solo from Letterkenny to Tralee and back north to Monaghan. The Monaghan footballer soloed ten miles each day to raise money for St Mary's GAA club in Castleblaney.

On Sunday, 1 March 1896, at Jones Road, umpires used coloured flags for the first time to show scores.

31

Bibliography & Index

Brehony, Martin, and Keenan, Dónal, *The Ultimate Encyclopaedia of Gaelic Football and Hurling* (Carlton Books, 2001)
De Burca, Marcus, *The GAA, A History* (Cumann Lúthchleas Gael)
Mahon, Jack, *A History of Gaelic Football* (Gill and Macmillan)
Mahon, Jack, *The Game of My Life* (Blackwater Press)
McRory, Séamus, *The Road to Croke Park* (Blackwater Press)
Ó Riain, Séamus, *Maurice Davin (1842-1927) First President of the GAA* (Geography Publications)
Rafferty, Eamonn, *Talking Gaelic* (Blackwater Press)
Smith, Raymond, *A Complete Handbook of Gaelic Games*
Sweeney, Eamonn, *A Pocket History of Gaelic Sports* (O'Brien Press, 2004)
The GAA Museum Teacher's Handbook

Websites
www.cul4kidz.com (the official GAA website for young people)
www.gaa.ie
www.scoilsport.org

Index (bold type denotes picture)